jBiog. MA SUL
Sullivan, Laura L., 1974- author.
Yo-Yo Ma : cellist

SEP 04 2020

P9-DBO-130

YO-YO MA

Cellist

Laura L. Sullivan

Cavendish
Square

New York

Published in 2020 by Cavendish Square Publishing, LLC
243 5th Avenue, Suite 136, New York, NY 10016

Copyright © 2020 by Cavendish Square Publishing, LLC

First Edition

No part of this publication may be reproduced, stored in a retrieval system, or transmitted in any form or by any means—electronic, mechanical, photocopying, recording, or otherwise—without the prior permission of the copyright owner. Request for permission should be addressed to Permissions, Cavendish Square Publishing, 243 5th Avenue, Suite 136, New York, NY 10016. Tel (877) 980-4450; fax (877) 980-4454.

Website: cavendishsq.com

This publication represents the opinions and views of the author based on his or her personal experience, knowledge, and research. The information in this book serves as a general guide only. The author and publisher have used their best efforts in preparing this book and disclaim liability rising directly or indirectly from the use and application of this book.

All websites were available and accurate when this book was sent to press.

Library of Congress Cataloging-in-Publication Data

Names: Sullivan, Laura L., 1974- author.
Title: Yo-Yo Ma : cellist / Laura L. Sullivan.
Description: First edition. | New York : Cavendish Square, 2020. | Series: Barrier breaker bios |
Audience: Grade 1-4. | Includes bibliographical references and index.
Identifiers: LCCN 2019016399 (print) | LCCN 2019017307 (ebook) | ISBN 9781502649713 (ebook) |
ISBN 9781502649706 (library bound) | ISBN 9781502649683 (pbk.) | ISBN 9781502649690 (6 pack)
Subjects: LCSH: Ma, Yo-Yo, 1955---Juvenile literature. | Cellists--United States--Biography--Juvenile
literature. | Chinese American musicians--Biography--Juvenile literature. | LCGFT: Biographies.
Classification: LCC ML3930.M11 (ebook) | LCC ML3930.M11 S85 2020 (print) |
DDC 787.4092 [B] --dc23
LC record available at https://lccn.loc.gov/2019016399

Editor: Alexis David
Copy Editor: Nathan Heidelberger
Associate Art Director: Alan Sliwinski
Designer: Christina Shults
Production Coordinator: Karol Szymczuk
Photo Research: J8 Media

The photographs in this book are used by permission and through the courtesy of:
Cover, p. 6 Larry French/Getty Images; p. 1 and throughout jorgen mcleman/Shutterstock.com; p. 3 and throughout Vecteezy.com; pp. 4, 20 The Washington Post/Getty Images; p. 8 Denver Post/Getty Images; p. 9 ©AP Images; p. 10 Don Bartletti/Los Angeles Times/Getty Images; p. 12 Draw05/Shutterstock.com; p. 14 ullstein bild/Getty Images; p. 17 Paul Marotta/Getty Images; p. 18 Scott Dudelson/Getty Images; p. 22 Bobby Bank/WireImage/Getty Images; p. 24 Frans Schellekens/Redferns/Getty Images; p. 25 Hiroyuki Ito/Hulton Archive/Getty Images.

Printed in the United States of America

TABLE OF CONTENTS

Yo-Yo Ma is a musician who breaks barriers.

CHAPTER 1

YOUNG YO-YO WOWS THE WORLD

Yo-Yo Ma is a famous **cello** player. A cello is a string instrument. It's played with a bow. The musician slides the bow across the strings. The cello is mostly used in **classical music**.

EARLY GOALS

Ma was born on October 7, 1955. He was born in Paris, France. His parents were Chinese. They were also interested in music. His father was a music professor. His mother was a singer. When he was

Yo-Yo Ma holds his cello between his legs.

seven, his family moved to New York.

Ma always knew he would be a musician. He just didn't know what kind. As a very young kid, he played piano, viola, and violin. He really wanted to play the double bass. However, that instrument is big. It's 6 feet (1.8 meters)

FAST FACT

Ma's cello was made in Italy in 1733. It is worth $2.5 million. It's nicknamed Petunia.

tall. It weighs 30 pounds (14 kilograms). It was too big for him. Instead, he was given a cello. A cello is 4 feet (1.2 m) tall. It weighs less than 10 pounds (4.5 kg). He liked it. By age four, he decided on the cello.

DEDICATION

Yo-Yo Ma had natural talent, but he also practiced a lot. Music was his passion. He practiced many hours each day. By age five, he was playing in public. At age seven, he played for two presidents. This concert was on TV.

He trained at the Juilliard School in New York City. Juilliard is one of the best schools for actors, dancers, and musicians. He later left New York to go to Harvard University. Harvard is one of the best colleges in the world.

Yo-Yo Ma and his sister are shown here performing in 1961.

At this time, Ma played at the Marlboro Music Festival. There, he met a woman named Jill Hornor. She helped run the festival. She and Ma fell in love and got married. They now have two children.

FAST FACT

Ma and his sister made up a musical distress call when their father was being too tough.

COLLEGE OR CAREER?

As a teen, Ma had a big decision to make. He was a brilliant musician. He could start touring and performing right away. However, music was all he knew. He wanted to learn more about the world. He decided to go to college first. He made education a priority.

Yo-Yo Ma went to college at Harvard before starting his career.

Ma studied **anthropology**. He said what a person learns before age twenty-one is like a bank account. They can make withdrawals from that their whole life. He knew his music would always be there. He put college first. That made him a more well-rounded person.

Yo-Yo Ma overcame many obstacles.

CHAPTER 2

YO-YO BREAKS BARRIERS

Ma had great success. However, he also faced many obstacles. One came when he was a young man.

OVERCOMING OBSTACLES

Playing an instrument is hard on the body. A cellist has to sit in one position. It can be very uncomfortable. Musicians must practice for hours. Playing can hurt the hands and wrists. It can also hurt a person's back.

Ma had **scoliosis**. Scoliosis is when the spine curves to the side. It can make a C or S shape. Ma's spine had an S shape.

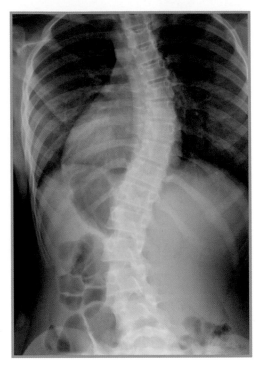

Scoliosis is a condition that curves the spine.

RISKY SURGERY

Scoliosis can cause pain. It can even be disabling. It makes less room for the lungs, which makes it hard to breathe. Ma knew he had to have surgery, but he also knew it would be dangerous. After surgery, he'd have to wear a cast. It would cover his upper body. He wouldn't be able to play for a long time. What if something went wrong? He could be paralyzed. This means a person can't move their body. Ma had to think about all these things before his surgery.

Ma had the surgery at age twenty-five. He was in a body cast for six months. All that time, he couldn't play his cello. He had played every day since he was four. This was a hard time for him, but finally, he could play again.

FIGHTING PREJUDICE

Ma also had to fight against **prejudice**. He was one of the first Asians to get famous playing Western classical music.

FAST FACT

When Ma was four years old, he and his sister would wake up at 4:00 a.m. to practice playing music.

Yo-Yo Ma was one of the first Asians to succeed in Western classical music.

Classical music came from Europe. It has a long history. The best-known classical music is from the eighteenth and nineteenth centuries. Classical music is written by a composer. Composers write exact notes. They also give exact directions. Unlike jazz or folk music, classical music is supposed to be played only one way. Before Ma, mostly white, European people played classical music.

MANY INFLUENCES

Ma was raised with different cultures—the customs of a group or country. His parents were Chinese. He was born in France. He later lived in the United States. People asked how a Chinese man could understand European music. Ma thought classical music was for everyone, but so was all other music. He decided he could embrace all parts of his background. Some

STUDY, THEN SUCCESS

Ma went to the Kalahari Desert in Africa to explore music from other cultures.

In college, Ma learned a lot about other cultures. He learned how other cultures use music. Some use it for entertainment. Others use songs to celebrate their history. Songs can be used to teach. Each culture uses music differently, but every culture has some kind of music.

Later in life, Ma used what he learned. He brought music from different places together. He blended styles. He showed people music they had never heard before. His early studies helped him succeed.

Yo-Yo Ma rehearses with the Boston Pops Orchestra in 2012.

people doubted he could do it. He had to practice very hard. He had to be the best and prove his ability.

FAST FACT

Yo means "friendly" in Chinese. In Chinese culture, a person's last name is written first. His name would be Ma Yo-Yo.

MUSIC IS FOR EVERYONE

Ma showed that people can choose what to love. It doesn't have to be from their own culture. He played all kinds of music. Ma proved that classical music isn't just for one kind of person.

Ma has performed with diverse musicians, like mandolin player Chris Thile.

Ma also showed that classical musicians could do more than play old European music. Ma never limited himself. He didn't just play the same pieces as everyone else. Instead, he played music from around the world. He played **tango** music from Argentina. He played traditional songs from China. He also played American bluegrass music. This allowed his playing to reach more people.

Yo-Yo Ma believes in music education.

CHAPTER 3

CLASSICAL MUSIC FOR EVERYONE

Ma has helped get lots of people interested in music. He brought classical music to people who had never heard it. He teaches people about new kinds of music.

REVIVING THE TANGO

Ma has recorded more than ninety albums. Not all of them are classical music. He likes to discover new music. He enjoys finding music that most people have never heard.

Ma has worked with the talented singer Bobby McFerrin, who is best known for his song "Don't Worry, Be Happy."

For example, tango is a lesser-known style of music. The tango is a dramatic style from South America. People like to dance to tangos, but many people don't listen to tangos. Ma found a composer who wrote many tangos. His name was Astor Piazzolla. Not many people knew him. Ma thought his songs were amazing. He said the music made him feel alive. Ma recorded many of Piazzolla's songs. Today, many people listen to Piazzolla's music.

SILKROAD

In 1998, Ma started a project called Silkroad. Long ago, the **Silk Road** was an actual road. People traveled on it to buy and sell things. They sold spices, silks, and other items. The road went through Asia, Europe, and parts of Africa. It brought many cultures together.

Ma helped revive the Argentinian tangos of Astor Piazzolla.

Silkroad does the same thing, but with music. It brings many musicians together. They perform music from their own countries. They also learn about

FAST FACT

Ma once left his cello in the back of a taxi! Luckily, it was found.

music from other places. Musicians in the Silk Road Ensemble perform together. They also discover new musicians. Part of their job is to teach students.

THE BACH PROJECT

Ma recently led the Bach Project. Johann Sebastian Bach was a composer. He lived in Germany. He lived from 1685 to 1750. Ma plays a lot of Bach's music.

Ma thinks Bach's music is important. It can reach all people in all cultures. Ma planned thirty-six performances around the world. He played all six of Bach's cello suites. He visited places on six continents.

The Silk Road Ensemble performs around the world.

A LOOK AT HISTORY

For a long time, many thought only white, European people could play classical music. A few people proved them wrong. Joseph Boulogne had an African mother. She was a slave. Boulogne's father was French. Boulogne lived in the 1700s. He was the first known classical composer with an African background.

Another groundbreaker was George Bridgetower. He was Afro-European. He lived from 1780 to 1860. He was an expert violinist. He became very famous in Europe.

These people—and Ma—set the stage for other musicians. Midori is a Japanese American violinist. She became famous in the 1980s. Today, most people know that anyone can play classical music. This is thanks to many people who broke barriers.

Ma has opened the door for new musicians. Now, people all over the world want to study classical music. He helps bring music to students in schools around the world. He also gives surprise mini-concerts. He has them on city streets. Many people can't afford tickets to his big shows. This way, they can still hear classical music.

Ma has several goals. He wants to bring beautiful music to everyone. He also wants to share cultures to build a better world. Music is a language everyone can speak. It can bring people together.

FAST FACT

Ma still practices every day. Sometimes it's for hours and hours. Other days, it's only for a few minutes.

TIMELINE

- **1733** Yo-Yo Ma's cello is made by Domenico Montagnana in Italy.

- **1955** Ma is born in Paris.

- **1960** Ma decides to play the cello.

- **1976** Ma graduates from Harvard.

- **1998** Silkroad is founded.

- **2011** Ma is awarded the Presidential Medal of Freedom.

- **2018** The Bach Project begins, bringing Bach's music to thirty-six places around the world.

GLOSSARY

anthropology The study of human society and culture through the ages.

cello A stringed instrument held upright between the player's legs and played with a bow.

classical music A style of music that began in Europe. The most famous classical pieces come from the 1700s and 1800s.

prejudice A negative feeling about a person or group felt for no good reason.

scoliosis A condition that makes the spine curve.

Silk Road An ancient trading route that went through Europe, Asia, and Africa.

tango A kind of music and dance popular in South America.

FIND OUT MORE

BOOKS

Angleberger, Tom. *Bach to the Rescue!!!* New York, NY: Harry N. Abrams, 2019.

Cham, Stephanie. *Yo-Yo Ma*. North Mankato, MN: Capstone Press, 2018.

WEBSITE

Classics for Kids: Music

https://www.classicsforkids.com/music.html

VIDEO

Sesame Street: **Yo-Yo Ma, The Jam Session**

https://www.youtube.com/watch?v=IRixaQ4hpEI

INDEX

Page numbers in **boldface** refer to images. Entries in **boldface** are glossary terms.

ABOUT THE AUTHOR

Laura L. Sullivan is the author of more than forty fiction and nonfiction books for children, including the fantasies *Under the Green Hill* and *Guardian of the Green Hill*. She lives in Florida, where she likes to bike, hike, kayak, hunt fossils, and practice Brazilian jiujitsu. Her favorite album by Yo-Yo Ma is *Soul of the Tango: The Music of Astor Piazzolla*, and she also loves all of his Bach recordings.